Where is My Father?

The Healing Answer for a Dying World

Dr. Aaron Williams

WHERE IS MY FATHER?

Paperback ISBN: 978-1-955605-91-5

Cover Design: Dr. Aaron Williams

Interior Design: B.O.Y. Enterprises, Inc.

Printed in the United States.

Acknowledgements

To my beautiful biological children, whom my wife Asia Williams helped me bring forth:

Alijah (AJ): You are my firstborn and beloved, who taught me so much about who I am and how I must grow. You are a leader to your little brother and sister. I love how you are embracing change while taking the initiative to lead. Way to go, champ! I love you for you.

Micah-Bean: You are a champion made by God. You remind me so much of the younger me, except you are your own character. You inspire me to keep going because cultivation comes through consistency and persistence. I love you so much.

Allie-Lee: You may be too young to read this now, yet you encouraged me to love from a different place in life. You were the promised child who came after seven years of prayer, trust, waiting, and wisdom between God, me, and your mom. I cherish your heart and desire to love you into a woman I can one day give to a man who will honor you for what God made you to be. I love you, sweet baby.

Asia: My sexy, one-of-a-kind lady. Thank you for giving me the gifts and the chance to lead my seed as you bore them. I love how you light up when you see me being a father to our own and to others in life. Let's keep growing together forever. I know we have much more parenting to do in this lifetime. I love you always, lady.

To my spiritual seed: Blessings to you, precious seed from God. I treasure your life and being able to walk with you. Thank you for receiving me and trusting God in me to help guide you into mighty spiritual maturity. We have work to do, and I appreciate this chance from our Heavenly Father for it. It's by His grace we can do this! I love you unconditionally!

Table of Contents

A Father's Quote:

"Guilt cannot change your past; any more than worry can change your future."

-Lonnie Curl

WHY I WROTE THIS BOOK

Years ago, after experiencing deep healing from what I call fatherless wounds, I felt strongly led to write this book.

I became convinced that people—especially men—needed a raw, honest, and authentic little "black book" that tells the real truth about fathers. Not a polished story, not a sugar-coated version, but a transparent guide that could serve as a tool for healing real pain. This book is meant to point us toward a clearer, healthier understanding of manhood and fatherhood.

But this isn't just for men. It's for anyone, regardless of gender, who is trying to understand the role and impact of fathers from a different perspective. Let's be honest—who grows from false information and surface-level answers? No one. Real growth requires real truth, spoken directly, yet given in love.

So, let's begin here.

If you're holding this book in your hands, it's likely that you either know someone who struggles with a broken or absent relationship with their father—or maybe that someone is you. If so, you're not alone. Let's walk through this journey together, and explore fatherhood through the lens of truth, experience, and healing.

A Father's Quote:

"Even though I've done good I always felt I could have done better, but at least they know I tried."

- Henry Chapman

CHAPTER 1: THE NEED OF A FATHER

Please understand this book wasn't written to insult or question anyone's manhood, worth, or value as a person. I didn't write this to shame fathers or accuse families. I know fatherhood is a sensitive subject. People often get uncomfortable, guarded, or even defensive when it comes up.

Have you ever noticed that? Ever wondered why? It's because the topic of fathers touches something deep…something personal, raw, and often unresolved.

The word father holds power. It can unlock joy or reopen wounds. It can stir gratitude or grief. And whether we like it or not, the mention of a father always leads us somewhere inside ourselves. That's because fatherhood is not just a social role, it's a soul connection.

It touches our identity, our direction, and our sense of worth.

The truth is our world has long suffered from the absence of fathers. I don't mean just physical absence, although that's a major part. I'm talking about emotional absence, spiritual silence, and relational gaps that have left many people young and old confused, angry, and lost.

Fathers are supposed to be the first reflection of identity and direction. They help answer life's big questions:

Who am I?

What am I worth?

Where am I going?

Am I safe?

Am I loved?

Without a father, or with a damaged connection to one, those questions often go unanswered. Or worse: they're answered by pain, pop culture, peer pressure, pride, or counterfeit love. In a father's silence, other voices become louder. And not all those voices lead us to truth.

This is why I believe we can't afford to just be mad about brokenness if we aren't willing to search for healing. We must seek truth. We must face the hard questions, including the one that titles this book: ***Where is my father?***

That question may not always be asked out loud, but it's there. It shows up:

- In the silence after a rejection.
- In the tears of confusion after another failed relationship.
- In the fists of a teenage boy who's never been taught how to process anger.
- In the ache of a girl who never heard her dad say, "I love you."
- In the striving of a grown man who never heard, "I'm proud of you."
- In the eyes of a woman who keeps choosing men who don't know how to stay.

This isn't just a personal issue. It's a global one. A generational one.

When fathers are absent or broken, everything feels the impact.

Marriages. Parenting. Education systems. Crime rates. Churches. Mental health. Even a person's view of God.

Studies confirm what the Bible already teaches: the presence of a loving, active father strengthens identity, security, and development. The absence of that father leaves a gap that almost nothing else can fill.

And here's the heavy truth: many men don't know how to be fathers because they were never fathered themselves. They were raised by women doing their best, or by men who were present in body but absent in spirit. They learned how to hustle, how to survive, how to avoid, but not how to lead, nurture, protect, or affirm.

So, the cycle continues. The next generation inherits the wounds and the silence. Until someone says:

"Enough. Let's do this differently."

That's what this book is. It's my decision to say "enough." Not in bitterness, but in boldness. Not in blame, but in love. Not to tear anyone down, but to build something better. I believe healing is possible. I believe restoration is real. And I believe it starts with understanding what a father is truly meant to be.

What Is a Father?

Before we talk about becoming better fathers or even finding peace with the one you had, we need to go back to the beginning. We need to ask: What is a father supposed to be? Not by the world's definition but by God's original design.

According to Scripture (even though some don't believe it), God is the first and perfect Father. He didn't just create fatherhood. He is Fatherhood.

- He is loving, yet firm.
- Present, yet powerful.
- Protective, yet gentle.
- Just, yet merciful.
- He sees us fully and still chooses to call us sons and daughters.

Psalm 68:5 calls Him "a father to the fatherless." That means even if your earthly father failed you or never showed up, there is still a Heavenly Father who will never walk away.

Even if you don't believe in God yet, I invite you to keep reading. I'm not here to force religion on you. I'm here to offer truth and hope. I believe once you start to understand who God is as a Father, you'll begin to see the difference between what you experienced and what He intended.

The Emotional Blueprint

When God designed the human heart, He wired it to respond to fatherhood.

- A father's words become a child's inner voice.
- A father's presence brings peace.
- A father's discipline gives structure.
- A father's affirmation gives confidence.
- A father's love reflects heaven.

Without that, we reach for substitutes—validation from strangers, attention through performance, power through aggression, or love through lust. We search in people what we were supposed to find in the one who gave us our name.

That's why this conversation matters. We can't afford to ignore the issue anymore. Because behind so many headlines, court cases, addictions, emotional struggles, and identity crises is a hidden question in someone's heart: "Where is my father?"

This Is for All of Us

And let's be clear: this issue doesn't just affect men. Women carry father wounds, too.

- A girl who didn't feel protected by her father may struggle to trust men.
- A woman who never felt chosen by her father may tolerate being used, just to feel seen.
- A daughter who never heard, "You're beautiful," from her dad may spend years measuring her worth by a mirror or a man's approval.

These are not just emotional issues. These are generational wounds. And the more we ignore them, the more they spread. I want to make it clear from the beginning: although this book is primarily written to help men and boys, it is just as necessary and valuable for women. In my experience, I've met many women who carry deep father wounds—just as many, if not more, than men.

If you're a woman reading this, I want you to know how important it is to understand your worth in the eyes of the Heavenly Father, especially if you've experienced the pain of an absent or distant earthly father. This isn't meant to insult or blame you, but rather to shine a light on a reality I've seen too often. A woman who has been deeply hurt by a lack of fatherly love can, without realizing it, carry that pain into every area of her life—including her interactions with men. Sometimes, that unresolved pain becomes a defense mechanism, a sharp edge that wounds even those who mean no harm.

Many women appear strong but carry a hidden bitterness that makes them guarded and hard to reach. They may not even realize how the absence of a father has shaped their outlook.

A woman who has not healed from her father wound might seem constantly angry or mistrustful, pushing people away, especially men who remind her of what she lost or never had.

These internal wounds can cause a ripple effect: broken relationships, repeated cycles of pain, and a deep struggle with self-worth.

Some women lash out in anger at the very people they love. I've witnessed heartbreaking situations damaged cars, damaged relationships, and damaged men… all as a result of a woman's unresolved pain. Others don't act out but instead carry a mindset that says, "All men are the same," shutting themselves off from meaningful connection and healing. This kind of reaction is often rooted in a deep father wound.

Sadly, this pain can be passed down to the next generation. A mother who hasn't healed may unintentionally pour her anger into her children. Sometimes the son becomes her emotional crutch, forced into a role he was never meant to carry. And often, the daughter absorbs her mother's pain and becomes twice as guarded, twice as bitter. These daughters may never marry, not because they don't want to, but because of the legacy of mistrust they've inherited. I've seen this firsthand in many cases over the years.

It's also common to hear some women say they are both the mother and the father to their children. While I understand the struggle and acknowledge that many women have had to raise children alone, the truth is that no woman, no matter how strong, can replace the role of a father. This mindset, though born from hardship, can lead to confusion in children. Boys and girls alike need both maternal and paternal guidance to grow into emotionally whole adults. When a girl grows up believing her mother was both parents, she may struggle deeply with her identity as a woman, especially when it comes to future relationships or marriage.

A father's presence gives a daughter the tools to navigate life with confidence and balance.

He helps her understand how to appreciate a man's strength while not surrendering her own value or boundaries. Mothers are essential, of course. They nurture, protect, and model womanhood; but they cannot teach fatherhood. Only a father can show a child what it means to be a man, to protect, to lead, and to love from that place.

Many women who struggle in marriage were never fathered as daughters. As a result, they may have difficulty trusting, submitting, or respecting the leadership of a husband, especially when he seeks to follow Christ. This isn't about control or inequality; it's about the spiritual and emotional balance that God designed. Without that foundational fatherly input, many women struggle to recognize or respond to healthy male leadership.

Now, this next part is difficult but important. I've worked with many people through counseling, ministry, and life in general including during my eight years in the military. Over the years, I've seen a pattern: some women, especially those identifying as lesbian, often carry deep father wounds. I say this with love and respect for all women, regardless of their sexual orientation. My goal is not to condemn but to offer a perspective born from many real-life conversations and experiences.

Some women say nothing happened to cause their orientation, and I respect their stories. But others, many who have found healing, have openly shared that their pain, especially related to absent or harmful fathers, contributed to their identity struggles. I'm sure you notice some differences we see in behavior today, such as women dressing like men, talking like men, etc. No matter how similar a woman seems to be compared to a man, she was not designed to play his role. This is why many same-sex relationships reflect much confusion internally and externally in how they're perceived. When a woman begins to reject her feminine nature or adopt behaviors traditionally associated with men, it can sometimes signal deeper identity confusion; confusion that often traces back to brokenness in the father-daughter relationship.

I know these are sensitive topics, and I say all of this with love. If you're a woman who identifies as lesbian, please hear me clearly: I love you in the love of Jesus Christ. My heart is for your healing and wholeness. You deserve to know the true, healed version of yourself—the one God created with care and intention. Sometimes, the lies we were told as children, "You're a mistake. I never wanted you. You're not good enough," can plant seeds of pain that grow into confusion, rebellion, or deep emotional wounds.

But there is hope. Healing is possible. Restoration is possible. And you are deeply loved by a Heavenly Father who will never leave or reject you.

You know the most paralyzing thing about the seed damage that happens to many? Most people don't feel they can get it out!

But we don't have to stay stuck in silence.

We can acknowledge the pain and still pursue peace. We can ask the question and still find the answer. We can look around at the brokenness and still believe something better is possible.

That's what this journey is about. It's about healing the inner child so we can lead as whole adults. It's about breaking the cycle, so the next generation doesn't have to carry our wounds. It's about rediscovering the true heart of the Father so we can reflect Him better in our families, our communities, and our calling.

So, if you've ever felt abandoned, overlooked, hurt, or just plain confused about fatherhood, this book is for you.

If you're a father trying to figure it out, this book is for you. If you're a man who never had a father but wants to become one, this book is for you. If you're a woman trying to heal from a father wound, this book is for you. Because no matter where you come from, you deserve healing.

You deserve truth.
You deserve a future that doesn't repeat your past.
Let's walk this road together.
Let's ask the hard questions.
Let's face the pain.
Let's rewrite the story.
There is hope.
There is healing.
There is a way forward.
Let's keep walking.

A Father's Quote:

"Know that I love you and you will one day have a family like the one God blessed me with."

- Chuck Miller

CHAPTER 2: DEFINING A FATHER

Before we dive into the practical and cultural understanding of what a father is, I want to acknowledge something deeply foundational: We cannot define a natural father without first acknowledging the Heavenly Father. He is Alpha and Omega—the beginning and the end of everything. He created fatherhood.

Our Heavenly Father is the greatest genius/artist behind all families. According to the book of Genesis, He designed fathers to lead, reproduce, and protect after His own nature. That means every function of earthly fatherhood was intended to reflect Him. But when this divine order is not established in a man's life, either by example or intentional teaching, something breaks.

Men become hindered from greater purpose. They lose their identity. And many fall into what I call "boy games" immature behaviors that sabotage their lives and hurt those around them. Make no mistake: this is not random.

There is an enemy: satan, the defeated antagonist of mankind, who hates fatherhood because it mirrors God's nature. He knows that strong fathers lead to strong families. So, he wages war against the family by first attacking the male to ensure he does not become a father. No, not every man is designed to be a father, though most are called to be one. The enemy desires to kill the seed in men who are potential fathers.

He does this through absence in the home. Through bitterness between parents. Through division, unforgiveness, and deep emotional wounds that plant seeds of dishonor and disunity in the hearts of children. This is why marriage, when honored by both husband and wife, is such a powerful weapon.

A healthy marriage built on mutual love and reverence for God becomes stable ground for the next generation. And that is exactly what the enemy fears. He knows that a home with a loving father in position spiritually, emotionally, and physically is dangerous to the kingdom of darkness. And this is not some biblical fairy tale.

Look around… we're watching this truth unfold in real time. Families are unraveling. Communities are hurting. Churches are struggling. Children are wandering. And so much of it traces back to the presence or absence of a father in his God-given place.

Have you noticed how many books and nursery rhymes center around "Mother Goose"? How often do you hear people talk openly and affectionately about their mothers? When I ask people about their childhoods, nine times out of ten, the first name or influence they mention is their mom.

But over time, this made me wonder: why is there so little conversation about fathers?

Why is it rare to hear healthy, public appreciation for them? Why aren't there more books about fathers, not just **dad jokes** or **fatherhood tips**, but real, honest, powerful reflections on the role of a father?

I started seeing how even systems around us are subtly shaped by this cultural mindset. When my wife and I had our first two sons, I quickly noticed how much of the hospital paperwork, care, and communication was centered on the mother. Rightly so mothers are carriers, nurturers, and deserve honor. But I couldn't shake the feeling of being pushed to the background. Even as I supported my wife and held my newborn sons, I often felt invisible in the process.

When we had our daughter not long ago, I saw it again. All the documents were addressed to the mother. Only one form even mentioned me. The room door had a tag with "Mother's Name" on it, but no "Father" section in sight. It may seem small to some, but these details reflect something bigger: a cultural default that sidelines fathers, even when they're present.

Let me be clear: I love and honor mothers. They carry a sacred and irreplaceable role. **<u>But honoring mothers should never mean erasing fathers.</u>** I believe God intended fathers to be visible, responsible, and deeply involved in the lives of their families. When a society begins to function as if fathers are optional—or replaceable—it begins to unravel at its very core.

So, What Is a Father?

To continue this journey, I want to talk plainly about what I believe fatherhood really is. It starts by asking one simple but powerful question: Who is a father?

That question haunted me for years. It rose in me during childhood, screamed in moments of pain, echoed through my sleepless nights, and lingered in my heart as I grew from a boy into a man. Every season of life whether I knew it or not, was shaped by the search for that answer.

Let's start here: a father is not just someone who produces a child. A man can be called a dad biologically, but that doesn't make him a father by responsibility.

The words "dad" and "father" are often used interchangeably, but I believe they are different in meaning and in weight. A father is not defined by what he creates, but by what he commits to. Fatherhood is not just production, It's protection, provision, presence, and purpose.

In its purest form, a father is:

• A man who takes his rightful place—given by the Creator—as the head and covering of his home.

• A protector who guards, both physically and spiritually, what God has entrusted to him.

• A provider, not just of money, but of wisdom, stability, correction, and love.

• A cultivator who nurtures growth in his children, shapes their identity, and prepares them for life.

This kind of man doesn't abandon when it's hard. He doesn't run when he's needed most. He shows up, not just in body, but in spirit, heart, and presence.

A father protects what he produces. That's the difference. That's what sets him apart from someone who simply contributed DNA. A father stands as a covering over his children, willing, even ready, to lay down his life if it means ensuring their safety and well-being.

What a Father Is Not

Now that we've begun to define what a father is, let's be honest about what a father is not.

A father is not a man who disappears at the first sign of discomfort. He is not a man who makes excuses to escape the responsibilities of raising the lives he helped bring into this world. He is not someone who lets culture, trauma, or his own past pain become a reason to remain emotionally unavailable.

I say this with respect to men who wanted to be better fathers but didn't have the tools. I say this with compassion for those who never saw a father model growing up. Many of us were raised in homes where the only consistent presence was our mother or another guardian. We didn't see what manhood was supposed to look like, let alone fatherhood. So, we learned by instinct, by imitation, or by desperation.

Some men never had the benefit of being taught how to be a father. They did what they saw. And often, what they saw was broken. But here's the good news: you don't have to stay in what you weren't shown.

The absence of a model doesn't have to be the death of your mission.

You may not have had a father, but you can still become one. You can break the cycle. You can relearn what fatherhood is by looking to the original model, God the Father. And for the one reading this who never knew his earthly father or never experienced his love, there is still a Father who has known you since before you were born. He has never left you. He is not like a man. He is not absent. He is not indifferent. He is deeply involved, even when you couldn't see it.

In Summary

Fatherhood is more than a title; it is a calling. It's not always loud. It doesn't always get applause. But its absence is felt in generations, and its presence brings healing to homes and nations.

Before we move to the next chapter, pause and reflect:

• What example of a father did you grow up with?

• Have you seen more of a "dad" or a "father" in your life?

• How has that shaped how you see yourself and how you see God?

A Father's Quote:

"Son, I know you're angry and we can work on that, but first, you will calm down and show respect."

- Lyndell Commander

CHAPTER 3: THE MALE CHILD

We've all heard the phrase: A mother's intuition is strong. And I agree, it absolutely is. But here's something I don't think we say enough: males have intuition too. Every young boy is born with an internal compass, a sense, a seeking, a quiet awareness that guides him through the world. It may not look the same as a girl's intuition, and it may not be as loudly expressed, but it's there. Deep inside a male child is a voice, a longing, a question often unspoken, but very real.

The difference is that girls are usually encouraged to explore those feelings, while boys are trained, directly or indirectly, to suppress them. We live in a society where boys are often expected to be tough, to "man up," to "shake it off." Vulnerability is not only discouraged; it's often punished. From an early age, male children receive the message that feelings make them weak, and silence makes them strong. This belief doesn't just shape childhood; it shadows manhood.

So let me ask you: when was the last time you heard a boy say: **I feel afraid. I feel left out. I feel confused, rejected, or disappointed.**

Probably not often if at all. But just because they're not saying it doesn't mean they're not feeling it. I believe boys are silenced long before they grow into men. Not always by abuse or intentional harm, but by neglect, neglect of their emotional development, neglect of their inner questions, and neglect of their need to be heard. Culture has taught us to accept the phrase, "That's just how boys are," as a blanket excuse for male emotional distance. But what if that distance is learned, not natural?

The Silent Cry

The truth is many male children suffer in silence. And silence, when left untreated, becomes suppression. Suppression becomes anger. Anger becomes confusion. And confusion eventually becomes self-destruction or destruction toward others. We often see the headlines of what men do; violence, addiction, incarceration but we rarely ask what that man was missing when he was still a boy.

What if we looked at the root instead of just the fruit?

Why did the boy act out in class?

Why was he fighting so often?

Why did he stop caring about school?

Why was he distant from home?

Too often, we wait until a boy becomes a man in crisis before we care about his emotional state. By then, it's harder, but not impossible to help him heal. I believe that if we had more conversations about male emotional health during childhood, we could prevent a great deal of the pain we see in adulthood.

My Own Childhood

I remember my own childhood clearly. By the age of five, I was already expressing behavior that raised questions. I said things I shouldn't have. I acted out. I disrespected teachers and challenged authority at times. There were moments I surprised even myself.

I was also charming, creative, and full of personality, but it was clear I needed correction. Not punishment, but understanding, guidance, and consistency.

The truth is, I didn't know how to explain my behavior back then. I didn't know what I needed. I didn't have the words to say, "I'm angry because I feel uncovered, or I'm confused because I don't know where my father is in all this." I just reacted.

To add, this is the time in my life when I started experiencing molestation by various people. This added to the layers of confusion and frustration I held inside.

But thank God for the mentors who eventually showed up. Some were teachers. Some were older men from the community. Some were family members who took the time to see past my behavior and help guide my heart. I will never forget the men who chose to speak life into me when they didn't have to. They helped me learn to listen, reflect, and grow.

**That's what every male child needs...
not just correction, but connection.**

A Culture That Must Change

There is a crisis in how we raise boys today. We assume they'll "figure it out" or that being quiet means they're okay. But I'm telling you—boys who are not guided will guess. And when a boy has to guess about his identity, worth, or emotions, he will almost always build on a broken foundation.

As men, we must stop passing down emotional silence as a badge of manhood. We must stop treating pain like something to hide and begin treating it like something to heal. If we want to raise better men, we must start by seeing the boys in front of us and hearing what they're not saying.

Before We Move On...

Ask yourself:

• When was the last time you really asked a young boy how he feels?

• If you're a man, what were you told (or not told) about your emotions growing up?

• What behaviors from your childhood were cries for help—but no one noticed?

Let's make it safe for boys to speak, safe for them to feel, and safe for them to grow. Because every man started as a boy. And every boy still carries the need to be fathered, seen, affirmed, and loved.

A Father's Quote:

"I just wanna love like Abba Father."

- Albert Epps

CHAPTER 4: ABSENCE

I want to make a personal connection with you in this moment by sharing the thoughts I had as a fatherless child. I didn't meet my biological father until I was around sixteen years old. But even after that long-awaited meeting, I realized something painful: I still hadn't found a father. This isn't to dishonor him, it's simply the truth of how I felt.

For years, I believed that discovering who my father was would bring me closure. I thought it would give me peace, understanding, and a sense of completion. I hoped that knowing him would finally heal the invisible wound I had carried for so long—a wound born not of a moment, but of a lifetime of absence. But instead of closure, I found confusion. Instead of peace, I found more questions than answers.

Growing up, I would often ask my mother about my dad. The answers would shift or point to different men. So, for much of my childhood, I believed someone else was my father. When I finally learned the truth, it wasn't just the loss of trust I had to process—I lost part of my identity.

I spent years attaching meaning and hope to the wrong name, only to find myself starting over, emotionally shattered and confused.

To anyone longing to find their father, I'd say this: talk to your Heavenly Father first. When I finally met my dad, he was incarcerated. I picked him up myself, believing that our relationship would begin to mend and grow. But I quickly discovered something. Although he was a grown man physically, emotionally, he was still the boy who got locked up years ago. He didn't have the mindset of a father. He had not grown into the role I hoped he would fill.

I'm not saying people shouldn't search for their biological parents. I am saying that prayer and closeness to God can help guide you through that search. The eagerness to find a father is natural, even beautiful. But it can also be dangerous if the father you're searching for isn't ready or capable of being found.

Fathers who have not been trained to love, to nurture, and to walk patiently with their children often end up wounding them further, even if unintentionally. I know God was telling me to be patient with my dad, and while I yielded in some ways, the little boy in me still longed for the moment I had missed all my life. I thought that his long absence would create in him a deep desire to be present. That was a painful assumption.

This is a tragic error in the soul of many today: we equate absence with eventual commitment. But absence, especially in immature people, doesn't automatically awaken responsibility. A person who hasn't acknowledged the damage they've done won't always feel the need to correct it.

Children need to be prepared for this reality. I believe it's healthy for a child to know as much truth about their father as possible because even when it's painful, knowing is better than wondering. I felt robbed when I finally found out who my father was. The absence made me feel blind…unable to see myself clearly. I mistook my frustration and confusion for normal feelings. But it wasn't normal. It was buried pain crying out for healing.

There is always a deeper search in a person who has a parent they don't know. That's what absence does. It doesn't just take away a person, it takes away clarity, security, and the identity that person was supposed to provide.

The Longing for Ownership

No matter what adults tell children about where their father is, that deeper desire to know the truth never fades. I remember looking in the mirror for years, wondering who I looked like. My skin color, nose, eyes, ears, and eyebrows made me ask questions. Do I look like him? Do I act like him? The desire wasn't just to have a father; it was to belong to someone. It wasn't about the title. I didn't want just any man's advice. I wanted the wisdom of the man I came from. I wanted to be able to say, "That's my dad." That longing was personal, powerful, and painful.

Now I understand why so many young boys resist guidance from other men who try to step in. That's where we get the phrase, "You're not my daddy!" It's not always rebellion, it's often a deep wound. A fatherless heart is a restless heart. And when that void goes unhealed, even genuine help can feel like a threat.

Though I saw my mother more than my father, it was my father's absence that haunted me most. And this absence doesn't only impact children, it scars adults too. There are men today who are fathers to children they don't have a relationship with. Maybe it wasn't their fault. Maybe they were kept away. But even if the situation is complex, the absence still eats at them like a parasite in the belly.

Is that my child? Where are they? Do they miss me? Will they reject me? The questions are endless. But there is a resolution: fight. Even if you feel it's not your fault, fight anyway.

Fight for your place in that child's life. Too many men give up, but giving up leaves a hole in that child's heart that no one else can fill not even God. Yes, God can heal, but He shouldn't have to fix what we were called to be responsible for in the first place.

The Power of a Father's Absence

Though my grandmother gave me love and stability, and I'm forever grateful, something was still missing. I now know what it was: I needed my father. Not just for discipline or provision, but for identity, affirmation, and guidance. A father's presence carries spiritual authority. He helps shape how we see ourselves, how we handle life, and how we walk in purpose. While our culture often elevates mothers, and rightly so, fathers are just as necessary.

Fathers are not optional accessories to the family. They are God-ordained pillars of strength, protection, and vision. That's why fatherhood is so powerful and why its absence is so painful. Absence is a poison that kills silently. A man can grow up, marry, have kids, and still feel a void he can't explain. The root of that emptiness is often fatherlessness left unhealed and unspoken.

Women, too, suffer deeply from fatherlessness. Many carry wounds of rejection, confusion, and identity struggles without knowing where they came from. But these roots are real. And they often begin in silence.

What I Witnessed in the Community

When I worked at the Boys and Girls Club, I encountered kids battling emotional turmoil. Many acted

40

out fighting, cursing, displaying shocking behaviors. And when I sat down with them and asked, why, the most common answer was, "I don't know." But with time and trust, the truth came out. "Only mom is home. Dad's not around."

I heard it too many times to count. These kids weren't just disobedient, they were hurting. They were growing up without the covering and correction that a father brings. In the community, and even the church, I've seen a growing number of young males embracing highly feminine characteristics. This is not a judgment. It's an observation.

Many boys, raised only by women, never saw healthy masculinity modeled.

I've known men who weren't gay, but who were often labeled as such simply because they mimicked what they saw: the women who raised them. But shame is not the answer. Presence is. We must raise up men, not just biologically, but spiritually and emotionally. We need mentors, role models, and spiritual fathers to fill the gap. Men need brotherhood and encouragement, not labels and rejection.

What I've Learned as a Leader

As a visionary in the local church, I've come to understand the human heart more deeply. My desire to lead people began early, but it deepened in the military. Both the church and the military operate on order and authority and when that structure is missing, chaos follows.

Look at Adam in Genesis 3. He was physically present but spiritually absent. His silence led to his wife's deception, their downfall, and the world's brokenness. Presence alone is not enough. Fathers must be active, involved, discerning, and protective. Inactive authority is just as dangerous as no authority. An active father raises a grounded family. And grounded families don't fall easily.

The Silent Needs

As I matured, I began to see the impact of my father's absence in new ways. I had gifts, talents, and leadership potential but I lacked the necessary tools for those things to flourish in my life. I needed a father to guide me. I felt it at school events, in conversations, and especially when watching other fathers show up for their sons. Seeing dads teach their boys how to work with their hands, play sports, or handle life was painful. I couldn't relate. It was always my grandmother who came. And while I appreciated her deeply, I still carried the same aching question: **Where is my father?**

Moments of Mercy

Despite the weight of absence, God sent people to step in at critical moments of my life. One of those people was my fourth-grade teacher, a white male who saw something in me and decided to invest time into helping me. I didn't know it then, but he was helping to fill a space that had been empty for years.

Later on, I got involved in acrobatics and dance, and the art teacher made time for me. She helped me find clarity and expression when I couldn't put my feelings into words. She may not have known the full impact of her presence, but I did. Those moments planted seeds of healing and confidence that I still carry with me today.

These men and women weren't my parents, but they chose to stand in the gap. And that made all the difference.

Before We Close This Chapter...

If you've ever dealt with absence, whether of a father, mother, or any key figure, I want you to know: your pain is valid. The loss is real. The questions are heavy. But I also want you to know that you are not alone. God sees the longing. He knows what you missed. And He is a Father to the fatherless. He doesn't replace your biological father. He fills the gaps no man ever could. He redeems what was lost and gives strength for what's ahead. Through His love, you can rise above the absence, and still become all you were created to be.

And one day, if you become a father yourself, you'll have the chance to give your children what you never had. **That's the beauty of healing. It breaks the cycle.**

A Father's Quote:

"Bad behavior left uncorrected leads to a ruined child."

- Henry Badie

CHAPTER 5: WHAT WE MAY NOT HAVE KNOWN

Damage in All People Unfathered (Spiritual Fathers)

I can honestly admit that through all the years of suffering from a father's absence, there is something unexpected I gained: wisdom and strength. That may sound strange at first. After all, how can abandonment ever produce strength?

But now, as a grown man and a father myself, I can see more clearly. I don't mean to rush past the word abandoned because that word carries weight. I used to talk about absence like it was just a missing space, but abandonment is something more... it's active, it's personal, and it cuts deep.

The Lingering Pain

Now that I have a family of my own, I realize that the effects of fatherlessness don't stay in childhood. They show up later, often in the most crucial moments when we become fathers, husbands, leaders, or when life challenges us to be emotionally available in ways we were never trained to be.

What we may not have known is that unfathered wounds don't always bleed immediately. Some pain shows up later, quietly hidden beneath the surface until pressure reveals it.

Have you ever felt emotions as an adult that seemed out of place? Ever reacted to something in a way that felt bigger than the situation? That's the aftershock of fatherlessness. I call it **delayed damage.** Wounds we thought we outgrew return in new forms... anger, fear of failure, emotional disconnection, perfectionism, or deep sadness we can't explain.

I've talked to many men who live with scars and current wounds even if they appear "put together" on the outside. Their pain traces all the way back to childhood. And too often, no one taught them how to deal with it.

Men, Ego, and Emotional Silence

One of the biggest challenges we face as men is ego. It's that quiet voice that says, "Don't cry. Don't talk. Don't need anyone." We grow up learning that expressing feelings is weak. So instead, we protect the pain instead of confronting it. And over time, that becomes our norm.

We suffer in silence. We bury our confusion.

We become fathers still carrying the weight of being unfathered.

And what's worse? Society is often OK with it as long as we're functioning. As long as we're working, providing, and staying out of trouble, the world doesn't ask us how we're doing on the inside.

But healing doesn't happen by performance. It happens by honesty.

Hidden Healing Spaces (Are They Healthy?)

I've noticed how men often find creative ways to express themselves. Barbershops, man caves, sports teams, gym locker rooms, fraternities, cigar lounges, online gaming chats, these are modern confessionals for many men. We feel safe talking around our pain, joking through our trauma, and sharing just enough to feel understood without going too deep. And I get it. Sometimes "something" feels better than nothing.

But here's my concern: are those spaces helping us heal, or just helping us cope? Yes, vulnerability takes trust. And yes, many of these spaces provide connection. But we must ask ourselves: is it healthy? Is it honest? Is it leading to growth? Or just temporary relief?

Just because a place feels safe doesn't mean it is safe. And just because a conversation feels good doesn't mean it's producing real change.

I've sat in barbershops where deep conversations were happening; life, relationships, fatherhood, and pain, but often, those moments get cut off before they reach the heart. The clippers stop buzzing, the laugh track kicks in, and the moment passes. Unfinished healing. Untouched wounds.

The Need for Spiritual Fathers

This is why spiritual fatherhood is so important. When we didn't have the father we needed, God often provides men who step in with grace, wisdom, and love. They may not share our last name, but they carry a piece of heaven's assignment for our healing.

A spiritual father doesn't try to replace your earthly dad. He simply helps guide, correct, affirm, and love you in ways that point you toward wholeness. These men might be pastors, teachers, coaches, uncles, mentors, or even friends' fathers who took the time to speak into your life.

I've been blessed to have a few father figures along the way, some I didn't recognize as such at the time. As I look back, their words, presence, and investment shaped me. Not all father figures are spiritual fathers.

The Bible says to honor older men and women as mothers and fathers, yet this is an honor for them as natural examples on the earth. They are built typically through time, with experience and wisdom to help equip the younger. However, they cannot replace spiritual parents. This is vital to know, especially regarding spiritual fathers. Why? Some people call elderly men their spiritual father, not knowing that they are not that unless God said so.

A spiritual father is one who is designed by God to father those he is assigned to by love, teaching (feeding), guiding, correcting, protecting, and modeling who Jesus Christ is in the earth.

Everyone is not a spiritual father. Wisdom and experience alone do not qualify a person to be such. A well-respected writer and apostle (sent man by God) of the Bible was Paul. He stated to a church that he was their spiritual father in the Gospel of Jesus Christ. He also said there are many instructors but not many fathers (see 1 Corinthians 4:15).

A big trick of deception in church is that people immediately depict spiritual fathering by age. They think older men are automatically candidates for fathering. This is an incredible mistake and has wounded many severely. Countless people, by study (survey and public admission), expressed how they were handed over to men as a child or adult to be spiritually fathered, but those men ruined them due to lack of capability to fill that role. In respect, though there are wise men walking the streets, they cannot replace a man who becomes a skilled teacher. The culture would probably argue wisdom is wisdom, yet that's not true. One must be equipped for specific works such as that. Regardless of age, God will use whom He wants, like He used Jesus as a young man to teach and spiritually father the disciples when He was on earth. Though many may not speak about this, it is evident that when the disciples left home, they needed a spiritual leader to love, guide, correct, and protect them. Jesus became this.

For example, when I had just married my wife and she moved in with me in our first year, God instructed me to spiritually father a young man who was a year older than me. I laughed and ignored it a little. He wouldn't let me go about it. See, in my teenage years God visited me through speaking to my heart about raising me into fatherhood and how I father the fatherless. I didn't know what that meant then, but I just accepted it and moved forward, keeping it a "secret" in my heart.

Well, it started happening quickly. It started in high school when the same guy I said God asked me to father was present and alone one day as I saw him from a distance. I heard God say inside of me, "You see him, go connect and guide him." This was different for me. I didn't really like it, but I knew it was God. It surely couldn't have been me. I felt strange approaching him to make a friendship that would later become discipleship. To shorten the story, I did it, and we became great friends.

Afterward, discipleship came. I was in the military, and I drove home one day to hear the Lord say, "Tell Ty (the man I'm speaking of), it's time for him to move from his home." In response he said he agreed yet didn't know where to. Next, God told me he was to move with me. I laughed, and while looking puzzled, I shook my head and didn't speak anymore until I got home. Once I got there, finding my wife standing in the living room, I asked her to meet in our bedroom. Before I could talk, she told me everything God said to me. Afterward, Ty moved in for a short period of time and was discipled and loved. We soon moved into a new home space, and he began using that home space for some time. Later, he helped me in ministry from day one and became the first spiritual son the Lord assigned to me.

It wasn't easy, but with God's help in humility and obedience, it worked/works!

Presently, Ty leads worship and other areas of ministry at the church that I oversee. He's also married and on a major path of victory in life! He's not the only spiritual son of mine, yet he's the first and is vital to me and my wife. His wife is also a daughter in the Lord to us. I tend to use their walk as an example, yet this does not neglect others we walk with in this way. You see, she didn't limit

God's desire to cause me to fulfill an assignment. I did not replace anyone's father. I don't take on roles of my own. God has to ordain and set men in place to lead spiritually, just as He did with the Apostle Paul.

Great confusion has come from this topic. The word spiritual alone stirs up issues for many who have not considered or embraced the need of a spiritual leader as father. I do understand. It can be extremely tough to receive someone if you do not understand their value or purpose to you. I notice that those who have had father issues of their own have a difficult time submitting to the spiritual fatherhood of another man outside of their father.

Common Mistakes of Those Needing Spiritual Fathering

– They accidentally try to make spiritual fathers their own father (hence, unrealistic expectations are created).

– Spiritual fathers mistakenly create more of a natural bond than a spiritual bond with those they are assigned to (i.e., they spend more time building natural relations than spiritual discipleship). This causes an overly casual mindset in the nature of most spiritual sons being discipled and, ultimately, if both aren't careful, it can taint the respect of the relationship.

There are those who are against spiritual fathering. They don't like the thought of someone being a father or spiritual covering. It's even believed by them that there is no biblical context for the term. However, the Bible is clear in the importance and critical need of a spiritual father. You'll find more of those details as you continue reading.

What Many Don't Know

Just like the absence of natural fathers can be damaging, the same is true concerning spiritual fathers. God created it that way. He knew many would not have their biological father. Whether alive or not, some fathers are not presently active. God knew this would happen and assigns spiritual fathers to help lead and guide those victims into victory and healing. See the importance of spiritual fathers now? We need these men. And one day, some other fathers will be an example like these men.

Maybe you're reading this, and you don't even go to church, so it might feel confusing or distant when I talk about God filling the hole in our hearts. I get it. But here's something I need to say clearly: God often uses people—especially men here on Earth—to carry out His work in our healing. He doesn't come down from heaven in person to do this job; instead, He sends people who reflect His love, guidance, and presence.

Throughout my life, God sent specific men to father me in different seasons, each one leaving a mark that helped restore what was missing. I want to honor a few of them now:

Mr. Miller, my fourth-grade teacher, was a Caucasian man who didn't just see a lost little African American boy. He saw me. He took me in like a son. I watched him love his wife with purity and respect, and it stirred a clean desire in me for marriage, even at the age of nine. That stayed with me.

Mr. Commander, my seventh-grade teacher, an African American man who was wild in the best ways, took me under his wing. He showed me that I was loved. From him, I learned the power of community and communication. He helped me approach the world with strength, respect, and grace. He gave me language and posture I didn't know I needed.

The late Pastor Henry Chapman was the first man to say out loud that he would father me; and he did. He corrected me in love, joked with me like a real dad would, and taught me the basics of manhood: how to tie a tie, how to treat a lady, how to carry myself with respect. Though I sometimes resisted his critiques, he helped shape the man I am. I'm better because of him.

There were others too.

And now, I must honor my current pastor, **Dr. Lonnie B. Curl Jr.** From the time I was 18 until now, he has pastored and mentored me with patience, wisdom, and consistency. He's been a pillar in my life, helping me grow spiritually and think deeply. He doesn't brag or ask for attention, but he deserves the honor of being mentioned here. He has modeled the faith, discipline, and character of a true man of God.

Each of these men, none of whom shared my last name, fathered me in ways that shaped my identity, softened my pain, and strengthened my calling.

Final Reflections

So, what we may not have known is that God always had a plan to repair what was broken. He placed these men in my life as spiritual fathers, to heal what was left aching.

And maybe…just maybe…He's done the same for you. Or He's getting ready to. Because spiritual fatherhood is real. It is powerful. And it is necessary. And if you haven't received it yet, I encourage you to remain open.

Healing rarely comes how we expect, but it does come.

One day, you may look back, as I have, and realize: you didn't just survive the damage. You were rebuilt. And you were fathered by the men God sent on purpose.

So, what are the next steps?

Has this book impacted you to a level of thinking to make a decision? I pray so. Whether you were/are the victim of being fatherless, or you are the father who's been absent, there's bountiful grace for us all. We need it to heal and to move forward. What I notice about fatherlessness is the mark it leaves on people throughout their life. Both the fatherless and the father who may have not been presently active in their child's life need healing to get where they belong.

It's interesting that Jesus was dying on the cross, and His most powerful words to be expressed were, "My Father, why have You forsaken Me?" This is interesting: in His humanity He felt left alone by God His Father. Yet the truth is He was not forsaken by God, though He was fulfilling an assignment that caused Him to temporarily feel the pain of what it feels like to be forsaken.

Yet the Bible says God won't forsake us and will be with us to the end of time. This is helpful to know—that even when we were rejected and alone, God kept us safe. How is that? The fact we are alive and able to continue our daily activities is a sign God isn't done with us and is helping us by breathing in us with the desire to bring us to our full purpose. Fathers need to know this. It's not too late to get things right. Sons should embrace this also.

Some fathers may never come to you and say they are sorry. If this is true for you, then you must know, like I had to learn, God the Heavenly Father will heal you and guide you along the way. It may not be easy, but you'll come out better than you think.

However, there are fathers, as I mentioned earlier, who may want to get it right and just didn't have the right teaching or a father to help them. They must be forgiven by sons whom they may have hurt. Forgiveness is a secret power that will unlock healing and bring peace and comfort to our souls.

In the Bible, Jesus' most powerful words about a world who hated Him and forsook Him were, "Father, forgive them; they know not what they do."

We must do the same for fathers who were not present for us or those who have hurt us badly. Let's forgive them. I know this may seem easier said than done, but it's the power that will bring immediate freedom. Many men I know have stayed angry and bitter with fathers that did them wrong, not knowing they only made themselves prisoners to pain, stagnation, and bondage for life. The best tool is to release people who have wronged us so that we can be free. God says if we don't forgive, He can't forgive us. It's not that He doesn't want to; He can't, because He's a God bound to keep His Word.

Can we pray now that we are at the final portion of this chapter? Just reverence Him, and I'll write what I'm praying just for you who are reading this.

Father, I pray now that the person reading this has received healing so far and will also grow even after this. May your anointing touch this now and free their minds or propel them, as needed, to affect someone near them who needs healing. Father wounds have hurt so many, and if they are in this category, Lord, please heal them now and show them there is a way out of bondage and into freedom for life! I ask for you to give them strength to release their pain and receive their gain in you. Restore relationships that you designed to be unified. Then also, sever what would harm them in relationships. After this prayer, may fresh spiritual birthing come alive inside them. May they experience the best life ever, which comes from you. Heal their seeds and future legacy right now, in Jesus' name.

A Father's Quote:

"Abraham, by faith, traveled to a land he knew not. In that journey he became a friend of God and the father of faith."

- Andy Clark

CHAPTER 6: GIFTS CAN'T FILL THE VOID

After observing many incredibly gifted people, those with extraordinary talents and abilities, I'm convinced that some believe their gifts can substitute for the healing they truly need. I was once in that position, and I learned that no talent can ever fill the deep void where wounds reside.

When we are hurt by people or situations, emotional wounds are created. These wounds take up the space in our hearts that should be reserved for peace, love, and purpose. Over time, if these wounds are not properly healed, they begin to stretch and fester, causing more pain and negativity to spread through our lives. This is why it's so important to understand: no matter how well we can sing, dance, preach, speak, play sports, or lead, if we are not healed, our brokenness will remain hidden behind our gifts, only to disable us further.

If you ask most people whether they want to be whole, I believe they'd say yes. However, if those same people are highly gifted, they might confuse their abilities with wholeness.

I cannot tell you how many gifted men, women, and even children I've known who struggle deeply with pride or depression, despite being the most talented in their circles. They carry an ability that clearly comes from God, yet their character suffers because they've tried to fill a void with their gift. This is why we see so many incredibly talented public figures who are broken behind the scenes.

From celebrities on television to people in our own communities, it's clear that many struggle to grow into their true identity because they've been led to believe their gift compensates for what's broken or missing within.

Take, for example, someone whose father was absent. If they are extremely gifted, they might convince themselves they never needed him. But if that wound goes unhealed, they grow into adults who feel torn inside, striving to appear strong yet lost in identity.

I've met countless preachers over the years who are amazing in the pulpit but privately wrestle with deep insecurity. That insecurity comes from unhealed wounds. It clouds their judgment and weakens their emotional sobriety. And when you live life half-sober, half-whole, it's only a matter of time before the lack of healing affects everything.

I say all of this with compassion. Life is hard, and we are all trying to make it through. But we must create space within ourselves for God to heal our wounds. That starts with admitting they exist and refusing to cover them up with talent.

You might be surprised how many people use their gifts to hide their brokenness. Some of the world's greatest stars have admitted, often before their deaths, that they lived behind a mask. They shocked the world by revealing their pain. I've even met counselors who counsel others with excellence yet silently suffer. I've known powerful speakers who articulate hope for others while internally dying from unresolved pain.

Many gifted people hide. It's natural, but dangerous. If that's you, I want to encourage you: stop using your gift to mask what only God can truly heal. Don't sing, preach, dance, box, or run over what needs to be surrendered.

Just like wrapping paper on a gift, the covering eventually comes off. And when it does, what's underneath will be revealed. I believe, deep down, we all want to be whole; not a broken image that only looks good on the outside.

You are loved. You can do this with God's help. Be honest. Seek healing. Get help. Be real.

A Father's Quote:

"I will raise you as a father and you will raise fathers."

-Your Heavenly Father

CHAPTER 7: PRESENCE

I sincerely believe that for every negative, there is surely a positive. A powerful piece of revelation God showed me in the scriptures blew my mind. Malachi 4:5-6 expressed that God would send Elijah the prophet to help turn fathers' and children's hearts back to each other. God asked me if I knew why. I waited on His perfect answer because, of course, mine wouldn't match. He said, "It's because absence is a curse, and if I don't have the prophet to help fill the gap, it would be a permanent curse." Oh, my word! Could you imagine absent fathers forever? That means the land would never heal. People would be damaged forever. A father's presence provides healing automatically. This is the grace God placed on fathers.

Instead of glorifying the power of father absence in our common communication, I believe we should shift our focus to the strength of a father's presence. This might not seem simple for everyone, especially for those who've grown up without that presence, but I truly believe it begins with having an open mind to receive a treasure that has the power to change lives.

The way we understand presence is key. **Presence isn't just physical. It's emotional, spiritual, and relational.** It's the engagement, the time spent, the undivided attention, the care, the protection, the affirmation—all of these combined create a presence that heals.

In order to appreciate the strength of a father's presence, we must first understand the damage caused by absence. Absence can be more detrimental than we often realize. When we've been deprived of something essential, the void can grow larger, silently shaping us in ways we don't fully recognize. But once we identify the damage, once we become aware of how it has impacted our lives, we are positioned to receive healing.

I want to draw your attention to the concept of presence in a different light. When I speak of presence, I am not merely referring to physical proximity. I'm talking about the kind of presence that fills the gaps of abandonment, the kind that provides comfort, security, and love in the most powerful ways.

The Healing Power of Presence

Can you ever imagine a moment when you were extremely afraid? I'm not talking about the typical anxieties of life but a deep, paralyzing fear that makes your chest tighten. Maybe you were standing at the edge of a decision you weren't sure about, or perhaps you were facing something out of your control. That fear often signals the absence of comfort.

It's fascinating that the Bible says, "Perfect love casts out fear." That's more than just a comforting phrase. It's a spiritual truth with incredible depth.

Think about it: fear cannot exist where love is present. And if we are talking about fatherhood, whether earthly or spiritual, there's a direct connection between the presence of a father and the casting out of fear.

A father's love is a protective force that reverses the insecurity and fear born from absence.

Absence and Presence: The Spiritual Connection

Now, I want to pause for a moment and reflect on something significant: we are all spirit beings, whether we believe it or not. Have you ever wondered why we dream, envision the future, or even sense things before they happen? Or how sometimes we know things we couldn't have possibly known, yet we just know them? That's the power of our spiritual nature at work.

Here's the thing I believe is true: the law of absence and presence is spiritual in nature. In the spiritual realm, the same way that absence creates a void, the right presence fills it. It's like pouring water into an empty glass. When the glass is empty, it cannot serve its purpose. But once it is filled, it is able to provide for others.

A father's presence in the life of his child is much like filling that empty glass. It is not just a physical space being filled but a spiritual and emotional space that enables the child to grow, to feel secure, to become confident in who they are. When fathers are absent, there's a growing spiritual and mental void within their children. It becomes a deep, aching emptiness that cannot be ignored.

The Void of Absence

This is why father absence has such a profound impact on the psyche and spirit of a child. Whether the absence is physical, emotional, or spiritual, it results in a void that

71

often manifests in unhealthy coping mechanisms, insecurities, emotional struggles, and difficulties in forming healthy relationships.

Imagine the child trying to navigate life without the grounding influence of a father's presence. It's not just about lacking a role model. It's about lacking the affirmation and direction that a father provides. The words that never came. The protective hand that wasn't there. The counsel that wasn't given.

This absence doesn't just create a longing for connection; it creates a spiritual deficit, a silent ache that remains throughout life.

That's why many people, especially men, struggle in relationships, leadership, or even their own identity. They are constantly seeking to fill a gap that was never addressed in their upbringing.

Fathers Who Heal

But there is good news. A father's presence can heal. When a father steps into his rightful place in the life of his child, whether his biological child or someone else he chooses to mentor, that presence brings restoration. The mere act of showing up with love and commitment begins to reverse the damage of absence.

We've all heard that "actions speak louder than words," and this is especially true for fathers. Words are powerful, but presence is even more so. Simply being there, offering support, guidance, and love can heal wounds that years of silence or absence have caused.

Embracing Presence

The challenge, though, is that many of us, especially as men, don't always know how to offer that kind of presence. It requires vulnerability, authenticity, and a willingness to embrace the role of protector, provider, and guide. It means more than just being physically present; it means being emotionally and spiritually available. It means showing up, not just in body, but in heart.

It also requires self-awareness. If we've been hurt by absence, we must recognize the void and begin the healing process. We must become open to receiving the healing presence of others, whether that's through mentors, spiritual fathers, or even our children.

We are all created for connection. Presence is the antidote to the absence we've experienced. The more we open ourselves to the power of presence, the more we heal and grow into the men, fathers, and leaders we are called to be.

Moving Forward with Presence

So, here's my challenge to you. Let's be the presence that heals. Let's not just talk about what's missing but also focus on what can be given. Let's fill the voids, heal the broken places, and restore the families, communities, and relationships around us.

Because in the end, **presence is not just about being there**, it's about making a difference when we show up.

AFTERWORD

As I come to the end of this journey, I want to leave you with a reflection on the power of what we've discussed throughout these chapters. *Where Is My Father?* is not just a question; it's a call to action, a recognition of the voids that father absence creates, and an invitation to embrace the transformative power of presence.

This book has taken us on a deep dive into the experience of fatherlessness, from the silent struggles of young boys to the lasting effects on men who carry the scars of a missing father figure. It has not been an easy journey, but it has been necessary. The wounds of father absence are real, and they shape who we are, how we interact with the world, and even how we see ourselves.

But this story does not end in pain. The absence is not the final chapter. What I've learned through my own journey and through countless conversations with others who have walked a similar path, is that there is healing, there is restoration, and there is hope.

The absence of a father is a deep ache, but it can be filled with the presence of fathers, mentors, spiritual leaders, and, most importantly, God Himself.

The journey of healing and restoration begins with acknowledging the absence, not as a permanent void, but as an opportunity for growth and transformation. It continues with seeking healthy presence—a presence that fills the gaps left by those who were unable or unwilling to step into the role they were meant to fill. Whether it's through the mentorship of another man, the embrace of a spiritual father, or the transformative love of our Heavenly Father, presence heals what absence has broken.

To the men reading this, especially those who have experienced the pain of fatherlessness, I want you to hear this: you are not defined by the absence you've known. Your story is still being written, and you have the power to change the narrative. You can become the father, the mentor, the man who shows up for others, even when no one showed up for you. You have the power to break the cycle.

To the women reading this, I encourage you to understand the profound impact that a father's presence or absence has on the men in your lives. Your sons, your brothers, your husbands… they need your support, your understanding, and your encouragement to step into their role as fathers, leaders, and men. The power of presence is something that affects us all.

As we move forward, let's remember that we are all called to fill the voids in our world—whether through the fathering of our own children or through the mentorship of the next generation. We have the ability to step into the lives of those who feel abandoned and to bring the healing presence they so desperately need.

Fatherhood is not just about biological ties; it's about being present, being engaged, and offering the love, guidance, and support that every person, especially every man, needs to flourish. We all have the capacity to be present. It begins with us. It begins with you.

So, wherever you are on your journey, whether you're still seeking, still healing, or already walking in the fullness of fatherhood, know that the power of presence will transform your life, and the lives of those around you. Keep showing up. Keep loving. Keep being present.

And most importantly, remember you are not alone.